50 NIFTY SUPER

More Science Fair Projects

By Natalie Goldstein

Illustrated by Neal Yamamoto

LOWELL HOUSE JUVENILE

LOS ANGELES

NTC/Contemporary Publishing Group

Published by Lowell House
A division of NTC/Contemporary Publishing Group, Inc.
4255 West Touhy Avenue, Lincolnwood (Chicago), Illinois 60712 U.S.A.

Managing Director and Publisher: Jack Artenstein
Director of Publishing Services: Rena Copperman
Editorial Director: Brenda Pope-Ostrow
Project Editor: Dianne Woo
Typesetter: Carolyn Wendt

Lowell House books can be purchased at special discounts
when ordered in bulk for premiums and special sales.
Contact Customer Service at the address above,
or call 1-800-323-4900.

Printed and bound in the United States of America

Library of Congress Catalog Card Number: 99-76524

ISBN: 0-7373-0368-9

RCP 10 9 8 7 6 5 4 3 2 1

Contents

Note to Parents and Teachers

For many students, creating and presenting a science fair project is a thrilling and confidence-building experience. Aided by the guidelines and suggestions in this book, children will plan and carry out experiments that answer science questions they themselves formulate.

Each project opens with a suggested question and hypothesis that guide the investigation. A list of inexpensive, easy-to-find materials is provided, followed by step-by-step procedures. Review the projects with your students or children and help them choose those that interest them. Help them in obtaining the needed materials and providing the necessary space and time to conduct the experiments. Be supportive of their creativity and natural curiosity, but resist the temptation to direct the project yourself. By organizing, conducting, and presenting their own investigations, children will gain a sense of accomplishment. They also will experience the excitement and pleasure of "doing science."

Getting Started

A science fair is an event at which students like you display presentations of their own science projects. These displays may include materials used in the project, colorful pictures or photographs, and charts and graphs depicting the results of the experiment.

Teachers or school officials usually are the judges at a science fair. Awards are given for the best projects and presentations. Even if you enter and don't receive an award, the experience is educational, rewarding, and, most of all, fun.

There are many kinds of science fairs. Some are organized by an entire school or by one grade or class. There are also city, county, and state science fairs. At the National Science Fair, held once a year, students from all over the country participate.

CHOOSING A SCIENCE FAIR PROJECT

First, you need to decide what kind of project you would like to do. What field of science interests you? Do you enjoy studying plants, the environment, weather, or chemistry? Choosing a project in a field you like will make your presentation more exciting and appealing.

Your project must involve a hands-on investigation that you do yourself. It must be practical—that is, easy to do at home, in school, or in your neighborhood, and the materials needed should be inexpensive and easy to obtain. You should be able to finish the project in time for the fair.

Your project should accomplish one of the four following results:

1. **Present research.** You create a display showing the method you used to collect data about your topic, as well as illustrations showing the results of your research.

2. **Demonstrate a scientific idea or apparatus.** You might show how a scientific idea—gravity, for instance—affects different objects. Or you might demonstrate how an apparatus—a pulley, for example—is able to move or lift objects. This type of project may include your own handmade model of a process or apparatus you investigated.

3. **Display a collection.** You display a collection of objects or pictures that helped you investigate your hypothesis. For example, you may have decided to investigate life-forms at the bottom of the ocean.

Your hypothesis may have been that since there is no light at the bottom of the ocean, most organisms there are blind. You can display pictures you collected of bottom-dwelling organisms to support or disprove your hypothesis. If you do a project on local geology, you may display rocks you collected in your area. (Simply displaying the rocks is not a scientific investigation. Your collection must show your attempt to answer a scientific question.)

4. **Do an experiment.** You perform a simple experiment at the science fair. Some of the projects in this book encourage you to continue collecting data by performing the experiment on people who visit your science fair display.

THE SCIENTIFIC METHOD

No matter what type of project you choose to do, it must be based on the five-step procedure known as *the scientific method*:

1. **Question.** Scientists observe what happens in the world around them. Every scientific investigation begins with an interesting question. Albert Einstein may have asked, "How does gravity influence light?" The question you ask will determine the purpose of your project.

2. **Hypothesis.** A *hypothesis* is a guess as to the answer you think you will get to your question by doing your experiment. Einstein's hypothesis may have been that very strong gravity bends light. It doesn't matter if your hypothesis turns out to be right or wrong. In science, a good question and a well-planned experiment are what's important.

3. **Test.** Once you have stated your hypothesis, you design and carry out tests, or experiments, to see whether your hypothesis is right or wrong. Your tests provide *data*—information that confirms or does not confirm your hypothesis. Most science projects include a *control*.

A control is part of an experiment that stays normal, or unchanged. If you are testing the effect of acid rain on plants, your control would be the plant that receives nonacid water.

4. **Record.** An experiment must be repeatable—that is, other scientists should be able to repeat the experiment exactly to test the results themselves. That's why it is so important to keep complete, detailed records of materials used, conditions (time, temperature, or other key variables of the experiment), how you conducted the experiment, what you observed, and the results.

5. **Conclusion.** When your experiment is finished, you must analyze the results you observed and draw a conclusion. Sometimes your conclusion supports your hypothesis; sometimes it doesn't. It's just as good to disprove your hypothesis as it is to prove it. The important thing is the process, or how your experiment was conducted. Perhaps your conclusion leads you to a new question and hypothesis, and a new experiment.

How to Avoid the "Silly Science" Trap

First, don't form a hypothesis that's too easy or too obvious: for example, "There are more birds in the park than in the parking lot at the shopping mall." Everyone already knows what the result will be.

Second, don't collect only the data that prove your hypothesis. For example, your hypothesis for the "STOP!" project on page 63 may be that teenagers driving sports cars will not come to a full stop at a stop sign. However, you may find that many do stop. Record ALL your observations, even the ones that don't support your hypothesis.

Finally, don't be discouraged if your hypothesis is disproved. Again, such an experiment may yield the most interesting and unexpected results and lead to new questions. Don't change your project because your hypothesis was disproved. In fact, science fair judges will likely be impressed by your respect for the scientific method if you include data that do not support your original hypothesis.

Always have the following equipment on hand when doing your projects:

- measuring cup and measuring spoons
- wooden spoons and metal spoons
- ruler
- masking tape and pen for labeling
- your experiment notebook and pen or pencil

SCIENCE FAIR RULES

You must follow the rules of any science fair you enter. Though rules may vary, there are certain guidelines that nearly all fairs follow:

1. All science fair projects must follow the scientific method.
2. Only one project is permitted per student, and usually only one student is permitted to work on a project. (An exception may be a fair that has a group category.)
3. Most exhibits can be no larger than 4 feet wide x 2½ feet deep x 6½ feet tall (1.2 x 0.75 x 1.95 m).
4. Projects must clearly distinguish between the work of the student and the work of others.
5. Projects must be set up and picked up during designated hours.
6. Students are responsible for the safety of their projects.
7. Exhibit backboards must be able to stand up on their own.
8. Exhibits using electricity must be designed to use 100 volts and are limited to 500 watts.
9. Exhibits must follow all local, state, and national laws regarding wiring, poisons, fire hazards, and general safety.
10. Projects cannot involve experiments on live vertebrate animals (animals with backbones: frogs, fish, birds, mice, etc.). Some fairs prohibit use of live invertebrate animals as well (worms, insects, etc.). Check with your teacher.
11. The following items are not permitted: preserved animals or their body parts, human body parts, microbial cultures, food syringes, pipettes, hypodermic needles.

CREATING A WINNING PROJECT

Judges look for originality in both thinking and presentation. They award students who show they understood and applied the scientific method. Judges want to see a project that reveals a scientific exploration you did on your own in a creative and scientific way.

The Written Report

Your report is a written summary of your project. It should describe each step you took from beginning to end. The judges want to know that you understand the scientific method, the scientific basis of your project, why you designed the experiment the way you did, and the results you got. Each step of the scientific method as used in your project should be explained in your written report. You also may include a table of contents, acknowledgments (in which you thank those who helped you), and a bibliography (a list of resources you used to get information about your topic).

Your written report should be typed on a computer or typewriter and neatly presented. Have the report handy at your science fair display so visitors and judges can read it.

Graphs and Tables

A graph is a picture that illustrates the results of your experiment. There are different types of graphs:

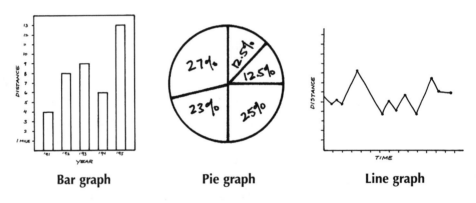

Bar graph   **Pie graph**   **Line graph**

A table organizes data in columns and rows:

Type of Car	Number That Stopped	Number That Slowed	Number That Didn't Stop
Sedan	10	8	0
Station wagon	9	4	0
Minivan	4	7	2

Making an Eye-Catching Display

Your project display is a visual summary of your project. A visitor to the science fair should get a good idea of what your project is about by looking at your display. Your display should stand out and attract the eye of visitors and judges. Creative use of signs, pictures, and color will enhance your display and attract attention. Remember that both pictures and written materials should be visible to those stopping at or passing by your exhibit. Here are a few tips for creating an eye-catching display:

NOTE

The flask in the upper right-hand corner of each project indicates the level of difficulty, from simple (1) to advanced (3). The approximate amount of time it takes to complete the project is also shown.

1. **Make your backboard colorful.** Paint it or cover it with fabric, burlap, or wallpaper. The color or covering should be attractive but should not overwhelm other parts of the display. At the top of the backboard, write your project title in large letters that can be easily read from a distance. The title should be 10 words or less. A humorous or clever title will attract visitors and judges. Beneath the title, post photographs, illustrations, graphs, and other materials that describe what your project is about and its results. Create your illustrations on poster board or color paper. Write easy-to-see titles on each illustration, and label important parts of diagrams.

2. **Attach brief explanations.** Write out these notes neatly and post them around your display so they can be easily seen.

3. **Use visual effects.** If your experiment is on plants, write notes on paper cut into leaf or tree shapes. Use three-dimensional models if possible; for example, build a model of a cell, display model cars, or make a crepe-paper model of a plant or tree. Make your display interesting and use effects that follow the theme of your project. Don't make your display too cluttered, however. And remember, it's the scientific content that's important.

4. **Make your display portable.** You must be able to set up and take down the exhibit easily. The backboard should be made of a lightweight material (thin plywood, cork, or foam or plastic sheets) and be constructed in two or three separate sections held together with hinges (available at any hardware store). Some stationery stores carry lightweight, three-sectioned foam core that is perfect for science fair displays.

There are 50 projects to choose from in this book. However, you may choose to use this book as a starting point for creating your own science fair project. You do not have to do a project exactly as it is described in the book. You can adapt a project to answer your own, original science question.

Each project is organized into sections. The Procedure provides guidelines to follow in designing your own science experiment. The question and hypothesis given at the beginning of each project are only suggestions. Think of a question you would like to explore and form your own hypothesis. Then design a method for testing your hypothesis.

Flower Power

Question: What substance added to water is best at preserving flowers?
Hypothesis: Aspirin will/will not keep flowers alive the longest.

When flowers are cut off from the roots, they must get nutrients from the water they are placed in to stay alive and blooming. In this project, you will determine which substance keeps cut flowers alive the longest.

Materials

- fresh-cut flowers of the same kind with at least 3- to 6-inch (7.5- to 15-cm) stems, one for each substance tested
- sharp knife
- vases, jars, or glasses, all the same size, one for each flower tested

- test substances (aspirin, sugar, salt, vinegar, milk, baking soda, cola, lemonade, toothpaste, or other non-toxic household substances)

Procedure

1. Have an adult trim the stems to the same length so that the flowers stick out of the vases. Each stem should be cut at a sharp angle (A).

2. Place each flower in a vase. Using a measuring cup, add the same amount of cold water to each vase.

3. Label one jar "Control." Nothing will be added to this jar. To each of the other jars, add one test substance and stir. Number each jar and label it with the name of the substance.

4. Keep a record of what substance was added and how much. For example, jar 1 got 1 aspirin; jar 2 got 2 teaspoons vinegar.

5. Place all the jars in a bright, draft-free area, out of direct sunlight. Record how the flowers look when you begin your project and each day afterward for 2 weeks. Count the number of petals that fall. Note when each flower begins to curl at the edges, wilt, turn color, or die. Continue to record your observations until only one flower is alive. What substance was in that jar?

Analysis

Some test substances you added contained chemicals that kept the flowers alive. Other substances you added may have killed the flowers quickly. What conclusion can you draw about how flowers respond to acids (vinegar) or bases (baking soda) in the water they take in?

Beaten Silly

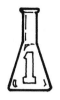

Question: Can a magnetized object be demagnetized if it is hit?
Hypothesis: Hitting a magnetized object will demagnetize it.

PARENTAL SUPERVISION REQUIRED
Magnetism involves the arrangement of atoms in a magnetized object. Can this arrangement be changed if enough force is applied?

Materials

- large iron nail
- large bar magnet
- paper clip
- compass
- block of wood, larger than the nail
- tape
- hammer

Procedure

1. Rest the nail on the magnet for 1 or 2 minutes to magnetize the nail. Note which way the nail is pointing.

2. Test the nail by holding it near the paper clip. If the nail is not fully magnetized, place it on the magnet again, pointing it the same way as in step 1, for a few more minutes. Test it again with the clip.

3. Place the compass on the table and turn it until the needle points north. Put the wooden block several inches from the compass so that its length is aligned east-west (A). Tape the nail to the block pointing east. Why do you think it must point in this direction?

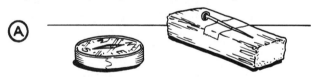

Ⓐ

WARNING

Never put a compass near or in direct contact with a magnet or magnetized object.

4. With an adult's help, strike the nail with the hammer 10 times. Touch the paper clip to it. Does the clip cling to the nail? Strike the nail another 10 times and test it again with the clip. Keep a record of how many times you had to strike the nail with the hammer before it lost its magnetism.

Analysis

When an object is magnetized, its atoms line up in clusters. All the magnetized north poles in the atoms point to Earth's magnetic North Pole. The more clusters there are pointing north, the stronger the object's magnetism. When a magnetized object is hit, the atoms are shaken out of their arrangement. Each hit jars more atoms out of line. If you keep hitting the object, it becomes totally demagnetized. (**Note:** The nail is pointed east so that it is not affected by the Earth's magnetism, which would happen if it were pointing north.)

What Transpires?

TIME
1 week

Question: Do leaves from different plants have different rates of transpiration?

Hypothesis: Plants with large leaves have a greater rate of transpiration than plants with small leaves.

Plants give off water through their leaves; this process is called *transpiration* (trans-puh-RAY-shun). You will determine if leaf size affects the amount of water given off by different plants.

Materials

- 2 green foliage plants of different types, such as philodendron (large leaves) and begonia (small leaves)
- clear plastic bags
- tape
- glass

Procedure

1. Try to test the same surface area of leaves on each plant. If your philodendron leaf is 3 x 6 inches long (7.5 x 15 cm), test the same surface area on the begonia. The leaves must all be on the same branch or stem. Measure the leaves to make sure the surface areas are fairly equal (A).

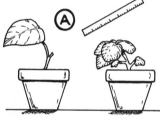

2. Carefully place a plastic bag over each area. Be sure not to break any stems or branches. Tape the bag closed around the stem (B).

3. Place the plants in a partly sunny window. Keep the surface of the soil moist.

4. Every hour or two, note the amount of water you see accumulating in each plastic bag. Count the droplets if possible. Record your observations for each plant for 1 week.

5. At the end of the week, carefully remove each bag. Pour the water into a glass and measure it with a ⅛ teaspoon. Which leaves produced the most water?

Analysis

Plants pull water up through their roots and into their cells through *turgor pressure*. When turgor pressure is low, the plant is not receiving enough water and will die. When turgor pressure is high, the plant is well watered, and the extra water is given off through pores, called *stomates* (STOW-mayts), on the undersides of the leaves. Some plants can hold more water than others.

Moving Magma

Question: How does magma coming to the Earth's surface affect the shape of the Earth's crust?

Hypothesis: Crust with huge rock formations is least affected by emerging magma.

The pressure inside the Earth is so intense that it produces enough heat to melt rocks into magma. Sometimes magma forces its way up to the surface as lava, which happens when a volcano erupts. You will create models of different kinds of crust and observe how magma behaves in each.

Materials

- several 10-ounce (312.5 mL) clear plastic cups
- scissors
- 1 or more tubes of toothpaste
- potting soil
- rocks, marbles, and other small objects

Procedure

1. Have an adult use the scissors to cut a hole in the bottom of a cup. The hole should be just big enough to fit the mouth of the toothpaste tube. Uncap the toothpaste and insert the mouth of the tube into the hole (A). The toothpaste represents the magma.

2. Fill the cup about ⅓ full of soil. The soil represents the Earth's crust.

3. Slowly squeeze the tube. What shape does the magma take? How does it change the crust?

4. Prepare more cups as described in steps 1 and 2. On top of the soil, add other materials, such as rocks or marbles, to represent different kinds of crust. Then repeat step 3 for each type of crust you create.

5. In your final test, prepare a cup with soil only. Have a helper press down on the soil with a second cup pushed inside the first (B). How does this change the shape of the magma and the crust?

Analysis

You saw what happens to magma when it pushes up against a thick area of rock. By holding differently shaped or arranged rocks on top of the soil, you saw how rock formations can make magma form different shapes.

Rock On

Question: How is sedimentary rock formed, and how do fossil imprints form in it?

Hypothesis: Sedimentary rock forms in layers, and imprints are saved as the layers build up.

Dinosaur footprints are imprint fossils found in sedimentary rock. Shells, leaves, and other objects create imprint fossils, too. You will see how sedimentary rock forms by making your own sedimentary rock. You also will make and preserve an imprint in the rock.

Materials

- 2 sheets construction paper
- blender
- white glue
- wooden spoon
- large mixing bowl
- strainer (big enough to fit across the top of mixing bowl)
- cookie sheet with sides; or large, rectangular glass baking dish
- newspapers
- cup with spout (e.g., measuring cup)
- shell or other object for imprinting

Procedure

1. Tear the construction paper into tiny pieces and put them into the blender. Add 2 cups (500 mL) water and 1 teaspoon (5 mL) white glue. Have an adult stir until thick. This is your paper mixture.

2. Place the strainer on the top of the mixing bowl. Pour the paper mixture into the strainer (A). Let it sit undisturbed for several minutes. It should be pourable, but not too watery. Do not let it become solid.

3. While the paper mixture is straining, put about 10 sheets of newspaper in the cookie sheet. Fold or cut the newspaper so it lays flat.

4. Pour the paper mixture into the spouted cup. Carefully pour a thin layer evenly over the newspaper. This is your first layer of sediment. Allow it to sit for several minutes until it dries a little. Test the layer with your finger: It should be moist but not wet, and it should not flow if the cookie sheet is tilted.

5. Pour several more layers on top of the first layer, allowing each to set before adding the next one. This is your sedimentary rock.

6. After the final layer is set, firmly press a shell or your hand into the sedimentary rock for one minute (B). Then let the rock dry completely.

Analysis

Sedimentary rock forms when tiny particles, or sediment, such as sand or silt, build up in layers over time. Silt is washed into rivers, and some of it comes to rest at riverbanks. If the river dries up, the layers of silt harden into rock. If you walk along a riverbank just before the rock completely hardens, your footprint might be preserved, just like the dinosaurs' were.

Turning Up the Heat

Question: How can you show how heated air moves?
Hypothesis: Shapes that spin in a circle will show how heated air moves.

PARENTAL SUPERVISION REQUIRED
You may have heard that hot air rises. But does it rise in a straight line?

Materials

- aluminum foil
- scissors
- small pinwheel toy (optional)
- needle and thread
- modeling clay
- 3 ceramic saucers or small dishes
- thin wooden dowel, about 1 foot (30 cm) long
- wire hanger or straight wire
- matches
- glue or strong tape
- 2 short candles

Procedure

1. Have an adult help you cut a spiral shape out of the aluminum foil.

2. Make a pinwheel by cutting the foil into pinwheel shapes and taping them together. Or, use a purchased pinwheel (remove the pinwheel from the wooden stick attached to it).

3. Use the needle to insert 6 inches (15 cm) of thread through the center of the spiral shape and the pinwheel. Remove the needle and knot the thread on the inside of each shape so it won't fall off the string. Tie a small loop in the other end of the thread (A).

4. Place a chunk of clay on a saucer and mold it into a block. Insert the wooden dowel so it stands upright.

5. Bend the ends of the hanger upward. Glue or tape the center of the hanger near the top of the dowel.

6. Hang one shape on each end of the wire. They should be at least 6 inches (15 cm) above the tabletop. Place a saucer under each shape, then put a candle on each saucer (B). Have an adult light the candles with a match. (Make sure the flames are several inches beneath the shapes.) What happens to the shapes?

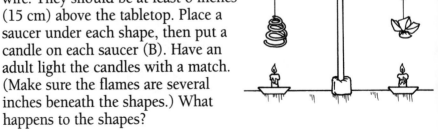

Analysis

When air is heated, it swirls upward. This movement is called *convection* (kun-VEK-shun). The convection currents you created caused the shapes to spin.

18

Plastic Fantastic!

Question: What household material can be used to make plastic?
Hypothesis: Milk can be used to make plastic.

Plastic is made out of very long chains of molecules called *polymers* (PAWL-uh-mers). You will use the chains of molecules in milk to make objects out of homemade plastic.

Materials

- clean, wide-mouth glass jar
- muslin or cheesecloth
- rubber band
- milk
- small pot
- vinegar
- waxed paper
- cookie cutter or other mold

Procedure

1. Cover the mouth of the glass jar with the muslin and secure it with the rubber band.

2. Have an adult help you warm 10 ounces (312.5 mL) of milk in the pot. Do not let it boil. Remove the pot from the heat and stir in 1 tablespoon (15 mL) vinegar. A rubbery white substance will begin to form. This is called casein (KAY-seen).

3. Strain off the casein by carefully pouring the milk through the muslin into the jar. Press with a spoon to squeeze all the liquid into the jar (A). The casein will stay on top.

4. Place a sheet of waxed paper over your work area and set the cookie cutter on it. Take the muslin off the jar and spoon the casein into the mold (B). Carefully push the casein to fill the entire shape.

5. Allow the mold to sit for several days until it dries and hardens. Putting the mold in a warm place will speed up the drying process.

6. To make a tree ornament or a piece of jewelry, use a safety pin to poke a hole through the shape while the casein is still soft. Once the casein is dry and hard, carefully pop it out of the mold. It can now be painted or decorated.

Analysis

Some plastics are made of chains 50,000 molecules long! The chains are tangled together, which is what makes plastic so strong. Milk, wool, and cotton also contain these long chains. Casein is used to make cheese and even glue. (See "Dairy Glue," page 84.)

A Ripple Effect

Question: What shape of stage has the best acoustics?
Hypothesis: An even curve will yield the best acoustics in a model of a concert hall.

If the music at a concert sounds good, that means the concert hall has good *acoustics* (uh-KOOS-tiks). The sound echoes evenly around the hall. Tanks of water are often used to test the acoustics in a concert hall, because the ripples in water are similar to the vibrations that produce sound.

Materials

- mixing bowl
- dark food coloring or black, water-based ink
- large baking tray (such as a lasagna tray), at least 1 inch (2.5 cm) deep
- 1 or more strips bendable metal, longer than the tray and 1 inch (2.5 cm) wide
- eyedropper

Procedure

1. In the bowl, mix the food coloring with water until you get a deep, dark color. Fill the tray with water to within about ⅜ inch (1 cm) of the rim.

2. Bend the metal strip into a curve and anchor it firmly in the tray.

3. Draw some water into the eyedropper. Position it just in front of the center of the metal strip. Carefully squeeze drops into the water, one at a time (A). Count "One, one thousand" (or whatever time you want) between each drop so they are dropped evenly.

4. Note the pattern and flow of ripples in the water. Draw a picture of it.

5. Take out the metal strip and bend it another way, then repeat the experiment. Bend it into a different curve, a V shape, an off-center curve, or a circle secured with tape. Draw the ripple patterns you observe.

Analysis

The water drops create a pattern of vibrations (ripples) in the water, just like vibrations in air create sound. Like sound, ripples usually radiate outward in circles from their source. If the shape of a stage in a concert hall is designed correctly, sound will travel in straight lines from the stage to all parts of the hall.

Sound Bouncers

Question: Which material is best at bouncing sound?
Hypothesis: Hard, smooth materials are best at bouncing sound.

A cave is a good echo chamber. Its walls are hard and smooth, and sound bounces off them in all directions. If you covered the cave walls with different materials, would they still be good sound bouncers?

Materials

- 2 stiff cardboard tubes, such as poster tubes
- ticking clock or watch
- test materials (pillow, smooth cardboard, wooden board, block of foam, fabric, dinner plate), each about 9 x 12 inches (22.5 x 30 cm)

Procedure

1. Arrange the cardboard tubes on a tabletop. They should angle toward each other, but not touch. Place the ticking clock at the open end of one tube.

2. Have a helper hold one test material upright on the table about 2 inches (5 cm) behind the close-together tube ends. Put your ear near the open end of the other tube. Can you hear the clock? Record the material being tested and what you hear.

3. Repeat step 2 for each test material.

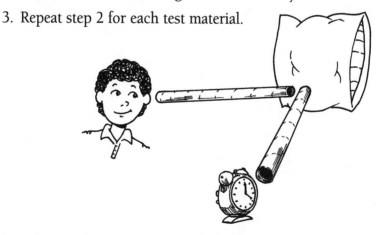

Analysis

Sound is air that is vibrating. When this air hits a hard, smooth surface, the vibrations bounce off. When it hits a soft, uneven surface, the vibrations are absorbed. You probably found that vibrating air traveled through one tube, bounced off the hard, smooth test material and into the second tube.

Make a chart showing which materials bounced the sound through the second tube loudly, normally, or softly.

Eggshell Power

Question: How much weight can eggshell halves hold?
Hypothesis: Eggshell halves will hold at least 10 pounds (4.5 kg).

Eggshells are very thin and break easily. But because of their shape and the way their molecules are arranged, they can hold an amazing amount of weight.

Materials

- 4 raw eggs
- bowl
- paper towel
- masking tape

- small scissors
- several books
- scale

Procedure

1. Gently crack open the small end of each egg with a metal spoon. Empty the yolks and whites into the bowl. (Keep the yolks and whites to cook later.)

2. Rinse each eggshell inside and out and set it on the paper towel to dry.

3. Carefully wrap a piece of masking tape evenly around the middle of the eggshell. Use the scissors to trim the edge (A). The tape will help prevent the shell from cracking.

Ⓐ

4. Place the four eggshell halves on a table, open end down, to form the corners of a rectangle. The rectangle should be large enough to hold the books you will add.

5. Weigh one book on the scale and record its weight. Place it carefully on top of the shells (B).

Ⓑ

6. Continue to weigh and add books until the shells crack or collapse. Keep a record of how many books you added, the weight of each book, and the total weight supported by the eggshells.

Analysis

Eggshells contain a mineral called *calcium*. In an eggshell, the molecules that make up calcium are arranged in the shape of a dome. Domes are one of the strongest shapes known. Any weight placed on top of a dome spreads down the dome's curved sides toward its base. Because the weight is spread evenly, a tremendous amount of weight can be supported.

You may want to use a sensitive food scale to weigh the eggshells. Then you can compare their weight to the weight of the books.

Variation

What would happen if you used the small end of the eggshell to support the weight of the books? Repeat this project with four new eggs, only this time crack open more of the egg until you are left with a small end.

Drop Race

Question: What effect does the surface of a racing track have on the flow of liquids in a drop race?

Hypothesis: The smoothest surface will make the drops flow fastest.

Different liquids flow at different rates. For example, ketchup flows much more slowly than water. In this project, you will test the flow rate of different liquids and see if the surface affects the rate of flow.

Materials

- books or newspapers
- pane of glass, about 8 x 10 inches (20 x 25 cm)
- 3 or more eyedroppers
- test liquids (water, vinegar, liquid soap, alcohol, cooking oil)

- stopwatch or clock with a second hand
- waxed paper, aluminum foil, paper towels, newspaper, sandpaper
- tape

Procedure

1. Stack the books about 8 inches (20 cm) high. Use a ruler to make sure the height is even all the way across.

2. Make sure the pane of glass is clean and dry. To create the racing lanes, place three pieces of masking tape at equal distances at the top of the glass. Label them "Lane 1," "Lane 2," and "Lane 3." Set the glass flat on a table.

3. Draw up one test liquid in an eyedropper. Put one drop about 1 inch (2.5 cm) under the Lane 1 label (A). Use the remaining eyedroppers to drop two other liquids under Lane 2 and Lane 3.

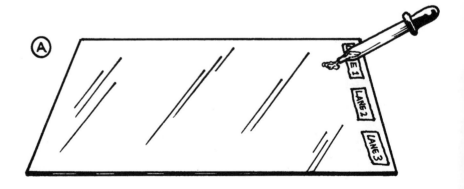

4. Carefully lift the glass and rest its upper edge on the stack of books (B). The drops will begin running down the glass. Use the stopwatch to time the rate of flow of each liquid until it reaches the bottom. Record the results. Which drop won?

5. Clean the glass and eyedroppers, and repeat using different liquids. Be sure to clean your equipment before testing a new liquid.

6. Clean the glass again. Cover the surface completely with waxed paper and secure with tape, and test the liquids again. Repeat the project with several different liquids and several different surfaces. Record all your observations.

Analysis

Different liquids have different *viscosities* (vis-KAW-sit-ees), or resistance to flow. Maple syrup flows more slowly and thus is more viscous (VIS-kus) than water. The surface on which liquids flow also affects their viscosity. Many liquids flow less easily on rough, resistant surfaces. Other surfaces absorb certain liquids.

At the science fair, have materials available so visitors to your exhibit can stage their own drop race.

Now You "C" It

TIME
several hours

Materials

Procedure

Question: What foods contain the highest relative level of vitamin C?
Hypothesis: Citrus fruit contains more vitamin C than other foods.

Your body needs vitamin C to stay healthy. But how do you know which foods contain the most vitamin C?

- cornstarch
- small pot
- glass
- 2 eyedroppers, plus 1 for each food tested
- tincture of iodine (2% solution, available at drugstores)

- test tubes and test-tube rack; or thin, clear glasses, one for each food tested
- test foods (tomato, apple, orange, and grape juices; soda; milk)
- blender (optional)
- white paper

1. Place 1 tablespoon (15 mL) cornstarch in the pot. Add water a little at a time and mix with your fingers to make a paste. Add 1 cup (250 mL) water to the paste. Have an adult boil this mixture for 5 minutes. Let it cool.

2. Put 5 tablespoons (75 mL) water into the glass. Use an eyedropper to add 10 drops cornstarch mixture. With another eyedropper, slowly add enough iodine until the mixture turns a dark blue or purple. This is your indicator solution.

3. Arrange the test tubes in the rack. Place 1 teaspoon (5 mL) indicator solution in each tube. Use a CLEAN eyedropper to add 10 drops of one test food to each test tube (A). (A clean eyedropper is required for each food.) Label each test tube.

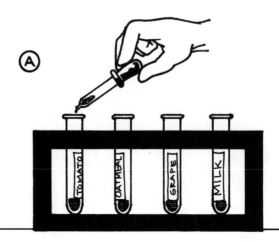

WARNING
Do not drink iodine. It is a poison.

4. Repeat step 3 for each food tested. If you are testing solid foods such as potato or broccoli, you will need to run them through a blender first. Add a little water to the blender to moisten the food.

5. Hold up each test tube against the white paper. Arrange the tubes by color from dark to light. The lighter the color, the more vitamin C that food contains.

Analysis

Vitamin C causes the indicator solution to lose color. The more vitamin C a food has, the lighter the indicator becomes. The chemical reaction that produces this change is an acid/base reaction. Vitamin C is ascorbic (as-KOR-bik) acid, which reacts with the indicator solution, which is a base. Create a color poster of your results, and graph the amounts of vitamin C in the foods you tested.

Bean There, Done That

Question: What effect do microwaves have on seed germination?
Hypothesis: Microwaves will hinder or prevent seed germination.

Microwave ovens don't harm the food that is heated in them, but the ovens must be carefully sealed to prevent the microwaves from escaping and harming people. You will determine if microwaves are harmful to seeds and prevent their germination and growth.

Materials

- empty foam or plastic egg carton
- 12 bean seeds
- microwave oven
- potting soil

Procedure

1. On the egg carton, label the first pair of compartments "0," the second pair "5," the third pair "10," the fourth pair "15," the fifth pair "20," and the sixth pair "25." This will be the number of seconds the seeds will be exposed to microwaves.

2. Fill each compartment with soil. In the first pair, place one seed about ⅜ inch (1 cm) under the soil (A). These are your control pockets. These seeds will not be exposed to microwaves.

3. Have an adult microwave two seeds at low power for 5 seconds. Plant these seeds in the second pair of compartments.

4. Microwave two more seeds for 10 seconds at low power and plant them. Microwave the remaining seeds at low power for the time indicated and plant them in the corresponding compartments.

5. Water all the compartments. The soil should be moist, but not soaking wet.

6. Place the carton in a warm, bright place, out of direct sunlight. Check it every day for 2–3 weeks and water as needed. Keep a record of what you observe each day.

Analysis

Microwave ovens use electromagnetic waves that penetrate foods and heat them from the inside. If microwaves penetrate seeds for a long enough time, the cells that make seeds germinate are destroyed. If a microwave oven is opened while it is in use, special switches immediately turn the oven off so harmful microwaves don't escape.

Can You Remember?

Question: Do we remember information better by seeing it or hearing it?
Hypothesis: Information is remembered better if it is received visually.

People and animals receive information through their senses: sight, sound, smell, taste, and touch. But sometimes one sense may help us better remember the information. You will determine whether sight or hearing is the stronger sense.

Materials

- 2 informational paragraphs (see step 1 below)
- paper and pencil
- tape recorder and blank cassette
- several volunteers

Procedure

1. Find or write two paragraphs on the same subject and at a fairly simple reading level. Both should contain specific information that is not technical; for example, names, dates, place names, events. Test the two paragraphs by writing out five questions for each. The questions should test the reader's memory. Have a friend read both paragraphs and answer the questions. If your friend correctly answers all the questions, proceed to step 2.

2. Type the first paragraph on a typewriter or computer and print it out. Type or print out your copy of the questions. Record the second paragraph by reading it clearly into the tape recorder.

3. Have each volunteer read the typed paragraph, then answer the five prepared questions that you read aloud to them. Then have each volunteer listen to the taped paragraph and answer the other five questions you ask.

4. Record the number of correct answers for the information that is read (visual) and heard (auditory). Repeat the test with as many subjects as possible. Test visitors to your exhibit at the science fair, too. Group your results according to male/female subjects, age of subjects, and so forth.

Analysis

Humans have a highly visual sense. In nearly all cases, information is better retained when obtained visually—as through reading—than when obtained through hearing.

A Winter Chill

TIME

2–3 days

Question: Do trees affect the temperature of the soil around them?
Hypothesis: Soil will be cooler in bare ground beneath evergreen trees.

Deciduous (deh-SIH-dyoo-us), or leafy, trees lose their leaves in winter while evergreen trees, or *conifers* (KON-ih-fers), keep theirs. Is the soil beneath leafy trees warmer than the soil beneath leafless trees? You will take the temperature of soil beneath different kinds of trees to find out what effect trees have on the temperature of the ground around them.

Materials

- sturdy thermometer
- tape measure
- wooden or metal dowel or stick
- field guide to trees
- watch

Procedure

1. Do this project in winter. Find a park, woodland, or backyard with trees that lose their leaves and trees that keep their leaves (identify these with your field guide). The ground should not be too frozen or covered with too much snow.

2. Hold the thermometer out in front of you for at least 3 minutes. Write down the air temperature.

3. For each tree you test, measure 2 feet (60 cm) from the trunk along the ground. At that point, push the dowel into the ground to make a narrow hole about 3 inches (7.5 cm) deep. Put the thermometer into the hole and leave it there for 3 minutes. Remove it and record the soil temperature.

4. Repeat step 3 for as many different kinds of evergreen and leafless trees as you can. If weather permits, do this experiment on a cloudy day and a sunny day to see how each affects your results.

5. Record what the ground around each tree looks like. Is it covered with a blanket of leaves? Is it bare? How does this reflect tree type and soil temperature?

Analysis

Deciduous trees lose their leaves to save energy, because it would take a lot of energy to keep their thin, fragile leaves alive during the winter. A conifer's needle-shaped leaves are coated with wax to survive harsh weather. The leaves dropped by deciduous trees cover the ground and act like a warming blanket in winter. Evergreen trees shield the ground beneath them, but the ground does not receive the same protective blanket of fallen leaves.

What a Gas

Question: What yeast food creates enough gas to blow up a balloon?
Hypothesis: Flour is the best yeast food and will create enough gas to blow up a balloon.

Yeast is actually tiny living organisms that grow and release a gas called carbon dioxide. When yeast feeds on bread dough, the gas it creates makes the bread rise. You will see which food helps yeast create enough gas to blow up a balloon.

Materials

- powdered yeast
- 2 glasses
- corn syrup, flour, apple juice, gelatin
- funnel

- 4 glass soda bottles, all the same size
- 4 balloons, all the same size
- tape
- tape measure

Procedure

1. Prepare the yeast in a glass following the directions on the packet. Or, empty three packets yeast into a glass and mix in 1 cup (250 mL) warm water. This is your yeast mixture.

2. Pour ½ cup (125 mL) corn syrup into the second glass. Add 4 tablespoons (60 mL) yeast mixture and stir thoroughly. Pour the solution into one soda bottle using the funnel (A). Label the bottle "Corn syrup." Wash and dry the glass, funnel, and tablespoon.

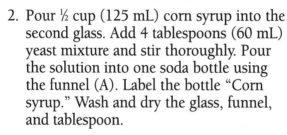

3. Repeat step 2 using flour instead of corn syrup, then using apple juice. Place each solution in a separate, labeled soda bottle.

4. Prepare the gelatin following the steps on the package and repeat step 2. Record how much of each ingredient you use.

5. Place a balloon over the mouth of each bottle. Secure it with tape so that no air can escape (B).

6. In a warm, safe location, lay the bottles on their sides. Check every half hour. Record what you observe. Hold each bottle upright and gently swirl the liquid. This makes the food more available to the yeast. Lay the bottle back on its side.

7. At the end of the day, which, if any, balloons inflated? Measure the circumference (the area around the middle) of each inflated balloon. Which was the best yeast food?

Analysis

The more edible food yeast organisms have, the more they eat and the more gas they release. Each soda bottle had the same amount of air and water, was kept at the same temperature, and had equal amounts of yeast and food. The only variable was the type of food. The quality of food was reflected in the amount of gas given off to blow up the balloons.

Variation

How does temperature affect yeast growth and production of carbon dioxide? Prepare soda bottles using yeast and the food they liked best. Put each bottle in a location with a different temperature (keep one bottle at room temperature as a control).

Take a Letter

Question: Is there a relationship between print size and remembering information?

Hypothesis: The smaller the print, the harder a reader must concentrate, and the more a reader will remember.

You can easily read through a first-grade book because the print is so large. However, you have to concentrate to read the print in a telephone directory. In this project, you will discover the relationship between print size, concentration, and the ability to remember information.

Materials

- informational passage (see step 1 below)
- computer with a printer
- several volunteers
- stopwatch or clock with a second hand

Procedure

1. Find or write a passage of about 250 words. The passage should contain specific information that is not technical; for example, names, place names, specific events. It should be at the reading level for your grade.

2. Type the passage into a computer (double-spaced). Print it out in a size 16 font. Print another copy at size 12. Print a third copy at size 8.

3. Write out five questions. The questions should test the reader's memory of specific information in the passage.

4. Give one volunteer 2 minutes to read the size 16 passage. Then read the volunteer the five questions. Record the number of correct responses. Have a different volunteer read the size 12 passage in 2 minutes, then answer the questions. Have another volunteer read the size 8 passage and answer the questions.

5. Test as many volunteers as you can, but make sure you have the same number of people reading each font size. If you have enough volunteers, group your results by male/female, age, and so on.

Analysis

Though you may think memory is best when the type is large and easy to read, that may not be the case. If the print is too easily read, the information is skimmed over and not remembered as accurately. If readers are forced to concentrate, as when the type is very small, they often retain information better and longer.

Slipping and Sliding

Question: What household materials make the best lubricants?
Hypothesis: The thickest liquids, such as motor oil, make the best lubricants.

Household lubricants are used to reduce friction between materials. For example, you would use a lubricant on the hinges of a squeaky door. In this project, you will test different substances to see which is the best lubricant.

Materials

- pile of books or newspapers, about 8 inches (20 cm) high
- piece of plywood, about 8 x 10 inches (20 x 25 cm)
- aluminum foil
- lubricants (motor oil, Vaseline, vinegar, baby oil, cooking oil, water, etc.)

- paintbrushes, one for each substance tested
- smooth block of wood, about 3 x 4 x 2 inches (7.5 x 10 x 5 cm)
- stopwatch or clock with a second hand

Procedure

1. Stack the books to a level height of about 8 inches (20 cm).

2. Cover the plywood with aluminum foil and wrap the foil around the edges.

3. Put 2 ounces (62.5 mL) of one lubricant in a measuring cup. Use the paintbrush to cover the foil with an even coat of lubricant. (If you have only one paintbrush and one measuring cup, wash them thoroughly with detergent before reusing them.)

4. Rest the top of the plywood securely against the books or newspapers. Hold the wooden block at the top center (A). The instant you release your hold on the block, begin timing its fall with the stopwatch. Record the lubricant used and the number of seconds it takes for the block to fall to the bottom.

5. Cover the plywood with a fresh sheet of foil and repeat, using a different lubricant.

Analysis

The more quickly the block reached the bottom of the plywood, the better the lubricant was at reducing friction. Thicker substances may make the best lubricants because they produce a thicker coating between two surfaces.

Frozen in Time

TIME

several hours

Question: Does adding different liquids to water change the freezing time?
Hypothesis: Liquids added to water will affect the freezing time of a solution.

Plain water in an ice cube tray will freeze in a fairly short time when placed in a freezer. What liquid mixed with water will allow ice to form in a shorter or longer time?

Materials

- jar or container
- freezer thermometer (optional)
- ice cube tray
- several glasses
- stopwatch or clock with a second hand

- test liquids (vinegar, ammonia, alcohol, dishwashing liquid, cooking oil, milk of magnesia, other non-poisonous household liquids)

Procedure

1. Fill the jar with tap water and let it sit until it reaches room temperature. Meanwhile, record the temperature inside your refrigerator's freezer compartment. (The temperature should be printed on a label inside the refrigerator. If not, place a freezer thermometer inside the freezer for a few minutes.)

2. Place 3 tablespoons (45 mL) of the room-temperature water into a glass. Mix in 3 tablespoons (45 mL) of one test liquid.

3. Pour the mixture into one ice cube pocket. Label the pocket with the name of the test liquid (e.g., "Vinegar") (A).

4. Repeat steps 2 and 3 for up to 10 more test liquids. In the last ice cube pocket, place 6 tablespoons (90 mL) room-temperature water only. This is your control.

5. Put the ice cube tray into the freezer and record the time. Every 15 minutes, check the tray. Write down what you observe about ice formation in each tray pocket. Pay special attention to the time at which your water-only control freezes. Continue until every pocket is frozen. (Tilt the tray gently to see if all the pockets are frozen solid or if some are still liquid underneath.)

Analysis

Different liquids freeze at different temperatures. When a liquid that freezes at a low temperature is added to water, the water will take longer to freeze. A liquid that freezes at a high temperature will enable the water to freeze more quickly.

Bad Hair Day

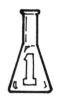

Question: Why does hair get frizzy on a humid day?
Hypothesis: Water vapor in the air makes hair frizzy.

On very humid days, your hair may get frizzier and look awful. In this project, you will explore what makes for a "bad hair day."

Materials

- plastic straws in their paper wrappers
- eyedropper
- glass of water
- wool yarn (optional)

Procedure

1. Hold a straw upright on a table. Tear open one end of the wrapper and scrunch the paper all the way down the straw (A). Carefully remove the scrunched paper and lay it on the table. Measure and record its length.

2. Draw up a little water from the glass into the eyedropper. Drop one drop on the scrunched wrapper. What happens? Measure the wrapper's length. Drop another drop and measure the length again. Observe and record the number of drops and what happens to the shape and length of the wrapper as each drop of water is put on it.

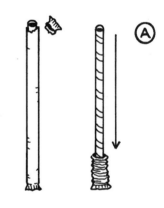

3. You may want to repeat this test with wool yarn. Wind the yarn around the straw, then push it down (B). Remove the yarn, keeping it scrunched.

4. Repeat step 2 with the wool yarn. Was there any difference between the paper and the wool? Did you have to add more water to the wool to achieve the same result?

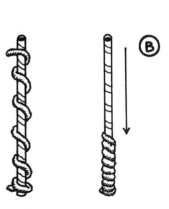

Analysis

Humidity is the amount of water vapor in air. Human hair absorbs water vapor. The water bends and twists the hair, causing it to get frizzy. The opposite happens when the air is dry. Wool is sheep hair. If you tried this experiment with wool yarn, you saw that wool absorbs water, just as the paper absorbed water. Both materials contain fibers that absorb moisture.

37

Color Crazy

Question: How do "color words" affect the ability to correctly identify colors?

Hypothesis: The printed color word affects the accuracy of naming the color in which it is printed.

The influence of the written word is so strong that it may affect our ability to name an obvious color. What happens when you see the word *blue* written in red ink? Find out!

Materials

- large sheet of white construction paper, 9 x 12 inches (22.5 x 30 cm)
- felt-tip markers or crayons in different colors
- several volunteers
- stopwatch or clock with second hand

Procedure

1. On the construction paper, write the names of basic colors using the markers. The color ink you use should be different from the name of the color. For example, write *blue* with a red marker, *green* with a yellow marker, *gray* with a green marker, *pink* with an orange marker. Write nine names in three even columns, with three words in each column. Do not repeat names, and do not use any one color marker more than once. Write the words in large block letters and fill them in.

2. Point to a word and ask a volunteer, "What color is this word?" (Remember, you are asking the volunteer to tell you the color that the word is written in, NOT to read the word itself.) Point to the next word and ask the volunteer to tell you the color. Give the volunteer 1 minute in which to name the colors of all nine words. Repeat with the next volunteer.

WHAT COLOR IS THIS WORD?

RED YELLOW BLUE ORANGE PINK PURPLE BLACK GREEN BROWN

3. Keep a record of the number of correct and incorrect responses for each volunteer. Record which colors or words they most often got right or wrong. Organize your results by age, and note if younger subjects (who are too young to read or are not yet very good word readers) are better at naming the colors.

4. Re-create the test sheet on a piece of construction paper big enough to display at your science fair booth. Test visitors and add their results to your experiment notebook.

Analysis

The Stroop Effect was named after its describer, J. Ridley Stroop, in the 1930s. The Stroop Effect shows how the brain processes conflicting information. When a person looks at the word *blue* written in the color red, two different types of information "collide" in the brain; this collision is called *interference*. The verbal interpretation (the word) often overrides the more basic visual information (the color).

The Nose Knows

Question: Is the human nose sensitive enough to tell the difference between different concentrations of a scent?

Hypothesis: The human nose can distinguish only between extreme differences in concentrations of a scent.

Can our sense of smell tell the difference between a solution with 2 drops of perfume in it and a solution with 4 drops in it? In this project, you will find out just how sensitive the human nose is.

Materials

- 4 or more clean, empty yogurt cups with lids
- 2 or more test scents (perfume or scent oil concentrate, cologne, orange juice, ammonia, vinegar)
- eyedropper
- several volunteers

Procedure

1. Pour 4 ounces (125 mL) water into each yogurt cup. In the first cup, put 3 drops of one test scent and stir well. In the second cup, put 6 drops of the same scent; in the third cup, 9 drops; in the fourth cup, 12 drops. Prepare at least four cups with varying concentrations of scent. (You can use any number of drops as long as they increase from cup to cup.) **Note:** You may want to test yourself first to see if you can detect any difference between the scent concentrations. Vary the number of drops you use in each cup and for each scent as needed.

2. Create a secret code that tells you the number of drops in each cup. This is so your test subjects will not know which cup contains more or fewer drops (for example, * = 3 drops vinegar, + = 6 drops, etc.). Label each cup with the secret code.

3. Repeat step 1 for the remaining test scents. Test at least two different scents; for example, a sweet-smelling perfume and a sour-smelling vinegar. Place the four sweet-smelling cups on a table. Make sure they are NOT in order of drop concentration.

4. Have a volunteer sniff each cup and tell you which contains the strongest scent (the greatest number of drops). Record the response. Repeat for each scent you are testing. For best results, test as many volunteers as you can.

Analysis

Alas, smell is not our most sensitive sense. We often need a great difference in concentration to tell which scent is stronger, or more pungent (PUN-jent). Some odors, like ammonia, may linger in your nose and affect your ability to detect different pungencies and scents. Though sense of smell differs from one person to another, you should have collected enough data to draw general conclusions about how well people detect differences between various kinds of scents.

Building Bridges

Question: What geometric shape and design structure make the strongest bridge?
Hypothesis: Triangles that distribute weight make the strongest bridge.

A well-built bridge should be able to hold a weight greater than the weight of the bridge itself. The materials used to build the bridge are formed into geometric shapes that distribute weight evenly throughout the structure, with no one part under too much stress. You will experiment with designs to build a bridge out of toothpicks and gumdrops.

Materials

- toothpicks
- large gumdrops
- string

- plywood ¼ inch (0.625 cm) thick, 14 inches (35 cm) long, 1¾ inches (4.375 cm) wide
- camera and film (optional)

Procedure

1. The bridge you design should meet the following specifications:

   - Total span 2 feet (60 cm).
   - Open span beneath: at least 8 inches (20 cm).
   - Roadway big enough to hold the weight of a model car.
   - Raised 2 inches (5 cm) above the table so that a toy boat can pass underneath.

2. You may want to research bridge construction, or look at pictures of different bridges to get ideas about what geometric shapes make a sturdy bridge. The shapes should be the kind that can be created using toothpicks and gumdrops.

3. Once you have a few designs in mind, create and connect the geometric shapes that form the bridge by sticking toothpicks into gumdrops. Experiment with different shapes to see which is the strongest. Use string to create cables to connect the upper parts of the bridge supports. Use a ruler to ensure your bridge measurements meet the specifications above.

4. Experiment with different designs until you create one that fits all the specifications. You may want to take photographs of each stage of your bridge construction. Keep a detailed record of the construction process: the shapes you created, how they are connected, and so on.

5. At the science fair, display your design plans and your finished bridge. Create posters showing how the shapes you created distribute weight throughout the bridge to make it stronger.

Analysis

If the weight on a bridge is supported by a single beam, the bridge will probably collapse under heavy use. Shapes that distribute or transfer weight to other supporting shapes are sturdiest. You probably found that toothpicks set at an angle into the gumdrops effectively distributed weight. You also had to create shapes light enough that gravity did not cause them to collapse. There are no "right" answers in this project, and there is no one way to build a bridge. The challenge is to find a good weight-bearing design using light, simple materials.

Fade Away

Question: What part of sunlight causes fabric to fade?
Hypothesis: The ultraviolet (UV) rays in sunlight cause fabric to fade.

You may have noticed that a sofa covered with dark fabric begins to fade if the sofa is in direct sunlight. In this project, you will try to discover which part of sunlight causes this fading.

Materials

- several swatches of black fabric, preferably upholstery fabric
- strips of colored plastic (red, yellow, blue, clear)
- tape

- scissors
- strip of UV-blocking plastic window treatment (available at hardware stores or on-line at Real Goods (www.realgoods.com)

Procedure

1. Cut the fabric and plastic strips to the same size, 3 x 6 inches (7.5 x 15 cm). Tape a plastic strip over one side of each fabric swatch (A). The clear plastic taped to a swatch is your control.

2. Cut a tiny piece of fabric only (not plastic) from the edge of each swatch and mount it on a record sheet. Label it with the color of plastic and the date (B). Keep your record sheets in a closed notebook or in a dark place. This is to prevent light from hitting the notebook and affecting your results.

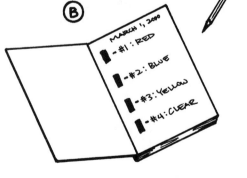

3. Place the swatches on a sunny windowsill. The window should get several hours of direct sunlight each day.

4. Check the swatches once a week for several weeks. Each week, snip a small piece from each swatch. Mount it on the appropriate sheet in your notebook and write the date. Observe any differences between the swatches. Continue checking the swatches until you see fading.

Analysis

We see colors because each has its own particular wavelength: red has a short wavelength, blue's wavelength is long. Sunlight contains wavelengths we cannot see, for example, those of infrared light and UV light. UV light can be very damaging; that's why we wear sunblock. UV light also makes fabrics fade by causing a chemical reaction. This same reaction causes sunburn and skin disease in humans.

Out of Sight

Question: How much tactile information is needed for a person to "read" a word using the sense of touch?

Hypothesis: At least half of each letter must be present to "read" a word using the sense of touch.

Braille (BRAYL) letters are made with raised dots that represent letters and letter combinations. Those who are blind "read" by feeling these dots with their fingertips. You will determine how much *tactile* (sense of touch) information a sighted person needs to read the letters that make up a word.

Materials

- large sheet of cardboard
- scissors
- pencil
- straight pins
- blindfold
- several volunteers

Procedure

1. Cut a piece of cardboard 3 x 5 inch (7.5 x 12.5 cm) in size.

2. Choose a simple three-letter word (*hut, dim, rid, sap,* etc.). Write it in pencil on the cardboard. The letters should be about 1 inch (2.5 cm) high.

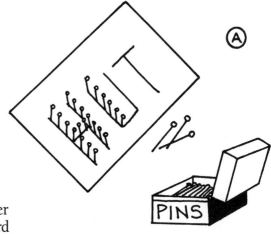

3. Stick pins along the pencil lines of each letter (A). The pins should be close to each other, but not touching. Keep track of the number of pins you use. This card is your control.

4. Cut another piece of cardboard the same size and write the same word in the same size letters. This time, use ¾ the number of pins to fill in the word. Space the pins evenly.

5. On the back of each cardboard, write the fraction of pins used.

6. Cut additional pieces of cardboard and repeat, using ½, ¼, and ⅛ the number of pins used in step 3. Use as few pins as you think will work for your project.

7. Before you begin the test, put all cardboard pieces out of sight of your test volunteers. Have one volunteer put on the blindfold. Present the volunteer with the cardboard that has the fewest number of pins. Ask the volunteer to use his fingertips to touch the pins (B). If he cannot read the word, present the cardboard that has the next greatest number of pins. Continue to present the cardboard pieces in this way until the volunteer can read the word. Record the number of pins needed for each volunteer to read the word.

Analysis

We depend heavily on our eyes for information, especially when it comes to the written word. A sighted person's brain is trained to interpret written words through the sense of sight. When words are presented through another sense, such as touch, the brain must translate the tactile information into a visual form (that is, it must get a "picture" of what is being felt) before it recognizes the form as a letter or word.

Variation

Did your results differ depending on the handedness of the volunteer? Does a right-handed volunteer more easily recognize a word felt with the right hand than with the left hand?

Metal of Honor

Question: What effect does acid rain have on different metals?
Hypothesis: Acid rain wears away most metals.

Acids react chemically with many materials. Acid rain wears away, or erodes, certain kinds of rock. Are metal structures immune to the effects of acid rain?

Materials

- small, clear glass jars, one for each material being tested, plus control
- test metals (2 copper pennies dated before 1983, 2 iron nails, 2 steel bolts, 2 pieces aluminum cut from a pie plate)
- white vinegar
- distilled water
- pH paper and color chart, or pH soil testing kit
- plastic wrap
- rubber bands

Procedure

1. Place one penny in a jar. Add white vinegar to cover. Label this jar "Vinegar." Put the other penny in a jar and cover with distilled water. Label this jar "Water."

2. Test and record the pH of the liquid in each jar. Dip the pH strip in the liquid for several seconds. Remove it and compare its color with the color chart. Record the pH indicated by the chart.

3. Cover the top of each jar with plastic wrap and secure with a rubber band.

4. Repeat steps 1 through 3 for each pair of metals you test.

5. Observe the jars every 3 to 5 days for 2 to 4 weeks. Record any changes you see in the metal objects. At the end of the project, dispose of all materials. Do not drink any of the liquids.

Analysis

At the end of 2 weeks, you may see color changes in some of the jars. For example, the acid in the vinegar reacted with the copper to form a bluish-green substance. If left alone long enough, the acid would continue to eat away at the penny, and the blue-green color would get darker. Eventually, the penny would erode completely. You may want to continue to observe the jars for 2 months to allow time for more easily seen reactions to occur among other metals you test.

Variation

How does the pH of the acid affect metal erosion? Use undiluted orange juice (a strong acid) and diluted orange juice (a slightly weaker acid) to compare.

Acid Rain

Question: What direct effect does acid rain have on plant growth?
Hypothesis: Acid rain will harm growing plants.

Acid rain often hurts plants by depositing heavy metals and other poisons in soil. The plants then take in these harmful substances with the water they absorb. But does the acid in acid rain hurt plant growth directly?

Materials

- 2 large jars that can hold 2–3 cups (500–750 mL) water
- distilled water
- white vinegar
- pH paper and color chart, or pH soil testing kit

- eyedropper
- 4 small glass jars that can hold 1 cup (250 mL) water
- 2 cuttings (stem and 1 leaf) each of philodendron and begonia or coleus

Procedure

1. Measure 2 cups (500 mL) distilled water into one of the large jars. Add 1 teaspoon (5 mL) vinegar and stir. Test the liquid's pH. The pH should be about 4. If it is below 4, add a drop of ammonia, stir, and test again. If it is above 4, add a drop of vinegar and recheck the pH.

2. Measure 2 cups (500 mL) distilled water into the other large jar. Test the pH. If it is below 7, add a drop of ammonia. If it is above 7, add a drop of vinegar. Recheck to ensure the pH is 7.

3. Pour 1 cup (250 mL) pH 7 solution into one small jar. Place one philodendron cutting in the jar. Label the jar "Distilled/philodendron."

4. Pour 1 cup (250 mL) pH 4 solution into another small jar. Place the other philodendron cutting in the jar and label it "Acid/philodendron."

5. Repeat steps 3 and 4, using the begonia or coleus. Keep the leftover pH 4 acid solution and the pH 7 distilled water solution.

6. Set the cups in indirect sunlight where they will not be disturbed. Check the cups every day. Record what you observe about each plant cutting. Make sure each stem is in liquid. Add more liquid (acid or distilled) as needed.

7. Note which cuttings begin to grow roots, and compare the growth of each. Draw pictures of each plant. Continue to observe and record the growth of the cuttings for 2 weeks.

Analysis

Plants grown in distilled water, which has a pH close to that of pure rainwater, should grow better and develop roots more rapidly than plants grown in a vinegar (acid) solution. The cells of all living things, including plants, are adapted to use liquids of a certain pH. If the liquid that enters the cells is acid, the cells may die or may not grow. In this project, the plant cells that would normally grow healthy roots do not function properly when they take in acid liquid.

Leaf It to Me

Question: Are tree leaves waterproof?
Hypothesis: Tree leaves shed water.

You know that trees take in water through their roots. But do tree leaves absorb the rainwater that falls on them? Or are they waterproof?

Materials

- books or newspapers
- 2 rulers
- paper towels
- 10 or more large, broad tree leaves (maple or sycamore)

- stick or pencil
- pitcher, glass, or jar

Procedure

1. Stack the books 4 to 5 inches (10 to 12.5 cm) high. Make a ramp by resting the rulers 3 inches (7.5 cm) apart on the stack. Place paper towels underneath (A).

2. Carefully arrange the tree leaves, top sides up, along the ramp. Place the first leaf at the bottom and overlap it with a second leaf. The center veins should line up. Continue until the whole ramp is covered (B).

3. Use the stick to press down gently on the center veins of the leaves (C). This will create a path for the water to flow.

4. Place more paper towels at the bottom of the ramp, in front of the bottom leaf.

5. Put water in the pitcher. Carefully and slowly pour a small stream of water on the center vein of the leaf at the top of the ramp (D). The path you made should keep the water from flowing off the sides.

6. Note and record the condition of the paper towels. Are the towels underneath the ramp wet? Are leaves waterproof?

Analysis

Trees and other plants get the water they need from their roots. If leaves absorbed water, trees and other plants would get waterlogged during heavy rains. That's why most leaves are waterproof. The leaves of maple trees have a pointy tip that helps water drip off the end of the leaf. Any unneeded water is released from tiny pores on the underside of leaves.

Variation

Try this experiment with other kinds of leaves. Double-check your results by seeing if the leaves float in water. If they float, they are waterproof. If they don't float, they absorb water.

The Coat Is Clear

Question: Does breaking a seed's coat help or hinder germination?
Hypothesis: Breaking a seed's coat will help it sprout.

Most seeds have a hard outer covering called a seed coat. This coat helps protect the seed until it lands where conditions are right and it can sprout. You will find out if breaking the seed coat helps or prevents a seed from sprouting.

Materials

- egg carton
- potting soil
- 12 bean seeds (such as lima, kidney, fava)
- sandpaper
- watch or clock with a second hand

Procedure

1. Fill each pocket of the egg carton with soil.

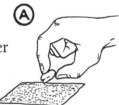

2. Rub the sides of two bean seeds with sandpaper for 10 seconds (A). Place each seed in a pair of egg carton pockets and cover with soil. Label this pair "10 sec."

3. Rub the next pair of seeds with the sandpaper for 20 seconds. Place them in the next pair of pockets and label "20 sec." Repeat for pairs of seeds rubbed for 30 seconds, 40 seconds, and 60 seconds (B).

4. Do not rub the last two seeds with the sandpaper. Place them in their pockets, cover with soil, and label "Not rubbed, control" (B).

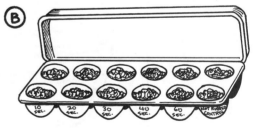

5. Water each pocket until the soil is moist but not wet.

6. Keep a record of each seed pair, how long it was rubbed with sandpaper, and what you observe in each compartment when you check it every day for 2–3 weeks. Wet the soil with water (but do not soak) as needed.

Analysis

Seeds are carried away from the parent plant by wind or animals. They may be tumbled among rocks or along the ground, battered by rain, or pecked at by birds before they finally land on a place where they can sprout, or germinate. The rough treatment helps break or weaken the coat. This causes the seed to sprout more quickly than a seed whose coat is not weakened.

Staying Fresh

Question: Does vitamin C prevent fresh food from rotting (oxidizing)?
Hypothesis: Vitamin C will hinder oxidation of fresh food.

Certain fresh foods, such as apples and bananas, turn brown and mushy when they are cut open and exposed to the oxygen in the air. Is there any natural substance, such as vitamin C, that helps prevent oxidation?

Materials

- mixing bowl
- chewable vitamin C tablet
- apple, banana, and pear
- knife
- slotted spoon
- several plates

Procedure

1. Measure 1–2 cups (250–500 mL) water into a mixing bowl (enough to cover the fruit slices). Place the vitamin C tablet in the water and let it dissolve (you may stir the water to speed up the process).

2. Have an adult cut the apple, core it, and slice it into four wedges. Quickly put two wedges into the vitamin C solution. Make sure the wedges are completely covered. Let them sit for about 30 seconds.

3. Use the slotted spoon to remove the wedges and put them on a plate. Place the wedges on their peel sides so that as much flesh is exposed to the air as possible (A). Place the two untreated wedges on another plate. Label each plate ("Apple + vitamin C," "Apple alone").

(A)

4. Repeat for the banana and pear. Peel the banana and cut it into chunks for testing. Halve the pear, remove the core or pit, and cut it into four wedges. Place each pair of fruit slices on a separate plate.

5. Put the plates in an area out of direct sunlight, where they will not be disturbed.

6. Record how the fruit looked at the start of the test. Then check the fruit every hour or half hour. Record your observations of the treated and untreated pieces. Leave the plates overnight and record your observations at several hourly intervals the next day.

Analysis

Fruit rots when exposed to air because the oxygen in the air reacts chemically with substances in the fruit. Vitamin C is an acid that prevents or hinders oxidation of fruit. It reacts with substances in the fruit that are not easily oxidized.

Variation

Would water alone hinder oxidation of fruit? Repeat the experiment, this time dipping fruit in plain water.

Righty or Lefty?

Question: Does handedness affect dominance (use and preference) of other parts of the body?

Hypothesis: Dominance of other parts of the body will be the same as handedness.

About 90 percent of the people on Earth are right-handed. But are right-handed people also right-eyed, right-eared, and right-footed?

Materials

- pencil and paper
- tennis ball
- penny
- paper-towel tube
- button (or other mystery object)
- small cardboard box with lid
- tape
- several volunteers

Procedure

1. First, test handedness. Place paper, a pencil, and a tennis ball on a table. Ask a volunteer to write his name on the paper (A). Record which hand was used. Ask the subject to throw the tennis ball at a blank wall. Record which hand was used.

2. Test for dominant foot. Place the tennis ball on the floor, away from the volunteer. Have him approach the ball and kick it toward a blank wall (B). Record which foot was used. Place a penny on the floor and have the volunteer cover it with his foot. Record which foot was used.

3. Now, test for dominant eye. Put a paper-towel tube on the table. Ask the subject to pick up the tube and look at something on a far wall through it. Record which eye was used.

4. Test for dominant ear. Out of view of the volunteer, place a button inside a small cardboard box. Tape the lid securely on the box. Place the box on the table. Ask the volunteer to try to identify the object in the box by shaking it. Record whether he holds the box up to the left or right ear.

5. Create a chart to record and tabulate your test results. What conclusion can you draw about the relationship between handedness and dominance of other parts of the body? Analyze your data for different age groups, for boys and girls, and so on.

Analysis

Handedness generally reflects the dominance of one side of the brain. For most people, their dominant hand is also their dominant foot, eye, ear, and so on. However, the brain is amazingly flexible. A right-handed person can learn to use the left hand as the dominant hand, and vice versa. If one arm, eye, or ear is injured, the brain can learn to compensate for such conditions, and dominance can be transferred to the remaining arm, eye, or ear.

Variation

The more tests you do for dominance, the better your results. What other simple tests can you perform to test the dominance of feet, eyes, ears, and so on?

Moldy Oldies

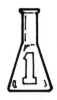

Question: Does food coloring affect the color of mold growing on bread?
Hypothesis: Food coloring does not affect mold color.

Mold is tiny organisms that grow on food. The mold organisms that grow on bread feed on the bread ingredients. If you color the bread, will the mold that eats it turn color also?

Materials

- several slices of white bread
- several plates
- several bottles of food coloring, different colors
- eyedropper (optional)
- plastic wrap or resealable plastic bags
- fork or pin

Procedure

1. Put one slice of bread on each plate. Color each slice with a different food coloring. Use only a few drops per slice. Use an eyedropper if necessary. Leave one slice of bread without any food coloring. This is your control.

2. Loosely cover each plate and slice with plastic wrap. Leave some air space around the bread. Have an adult use a fork or pin to poke a few holes in the top of the plastic to let in more air (A).

3. Set the plates where they will not be disturbed. Observe the bread on each plate every day for 2 weeks, or until mold is growing. Record what you observe on each slice. Did the food coloring affect how quickly mold grew? Did it affect the color of the mold? What color was the mold on the control slice?

Analysis

The air around us is filled with many kinds of invisible organisms. Some of these are molds, which feed on and decay different foods. Some molds grow on old cheese, others grow on fruits or bread. Many bread molds are green. Adding food coloring should not affect the color of the mold. The mold has its own coloring.

Variation

Repeat this experiment with whole wheat bread or dark brown pumpernickel bread. Test mold color and growth on small chunks of different cheeses wrapped in plastic. Allow the mold to grow for several weeks. How does cheese mold differ from bread mold? What color is it? Does adding food coloring to cheese (or does the color of the cheese) affect the color of the mold?

33 Keeping in Touch

Question: How sensitive to touch are different parts of the body?
Hypothesis: Some parts of the body are more sensitive to touch than others.

Which are more sensitive to touch: your fingertips or the soles of your feet? You probably would say your fingertips. But how sensitive are other parts of your body?

Materials

- monofilament fishing line in three different thicknesses (available at sporting goods or hardware stores), a few inches each
- 3 Popsicle sticks or small (6-inch) rulers
- tape or glue
- scissors
- blindfold
- several volunteers

Procedure

1. From each fishing line, cut a piece 1.5 inches (3.75 cm) long. Tape or glue one end of each line to one end of a Popsicle stick. About 1 inch (2.5 cm) should hang down perpendicular to the stick (A).

2. One at a time, have the volunteers put on the blindfold. Touch the thinnest fishing line to their forearms until the hairs bend (B). Ask if they felt anything. If not, touch the next thickest line to the same area. If nothing is felt, try the thickest line. Record the thickness of fishing line used and each subject's response.

3. Test various parts of the body: forearm, shoulder, back of hand, elbow, top of foot, knee. Always begin with the thinnest fishing line. Always test on bare skin, not through clothing. Record all results. You may want to group your results according to age, boy/girl, and so on.

Analysis

You performed a test similar to one used by *neurologists* (nur-OL-oh-jists), doctors who specialize in diseases of the nervous system. Neurologists call this the *Von Frey* (vuhn FRY) *Hairs* test. It helps determine if nerves in different parts of the body are damaged and no longer sense touch the way they should. When you organize the results of your testing, you will likely see that different parts of a healthy body have different sensitivity to touch.

Stop!

Question: How do different drivers behave at a stop sign?
Hypothesis: Most drivers come to a full stop at a stop sign.

Stop signs are meant to ensure people's safety. Yet, as we all have observed, not everyone comes to a full stop at a stop sign. You will monitor one or more stop signs and observe different categories of drivers and how they behave.

Materials

- pencil and notebook
- watch

Procedure

1. Locate a stop sign on a corner in your neighborhood. In your notebook, record the type of area the sign is in, for example, a busy business district or a quiet neighborhood.

2. With your pencil and notebook in hand, observe and record how different drivers behave. Tally how many drivers come to a full stop, how many slow down and roll past the sign, and how many drive through the sign without slowing.

3. Observe traffic for periods of no less than 15 minutes at a time. If possible, observe the traffic at different times of day (rush hour, mid-afternoon), on different days (weekdays, weekends), and in different parts of town that get different kinds of traffic (business, residential).

4. Keep a record of other categories: if the driver is a man or a woman; age (teenager, older person); type of vehicle (sports car, station wagon, minivan, truck). There are many different categories of data you can collect.

5. Tally your results and analyze your data for each category you created.

Analysis

Human behavior varies considerably, especially when people are behind the wheel of an automobile. There is no one "right" result for this project, but you should get some interesting insights into how people behave when faced with rules such as stop signs. The most interesting results may come from correlations between type of car driven, age of driver, and behavior at a stop sign.

Fatty Padding

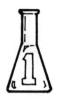

Question: Does fat help keep animals warm?
Hypothesis: Fat is a good insulator and helps keep animals warm.

How do penguins stay warm in a place as cold as the South Pole? Does the fat under their skin keep them warm? In this project, you will find out if fat is a good insulator—that is, if it helps animals maintain their body temperature.

Materials

- 4 thermometers
- 2 drinking glasses, about 2 inches (5 cm) in diameter
- shortening

- thin glass jar, such as a spice jar, about 1 inch (2.5 cm) in diameter

Procedure

1. An hour before you begin the experiment, place a thermometer in the freezer. After an hour, record the freezer temperature.

2. Fill one drinking glass with shortening. Tamp it down with a spoon to make sure there are no air spaces in it. This represents your fatty insulation.

3. Record the room temperature on the second thermometer. Insert the thermometer into the center of the shortening. Stand it upright so it is not touching the side of the glass.

4. Measure and record the distance between the thermometer and the side of the glass (A). This is the thickness of the fatty insulation.

5. Fill the spice jar with shortening. Record the room temperature on the third thermometer and place it upright in the center of the shortening. Measure and record the thickness of the insulation.

6. Record the room temperature on the fourth thermometer and place it in the empty second drinking glass. This is your control.

7. Place all three glasses, with thermometers, in the freezer. Check and record their temperatures every 5 minutes for half an hour. Which thermometer showed the least temperature loss? Which was in the best insulation?

Analysis

Fat is a good insulator. The more fat a body can accumulate under the skin, the better insulated the body is. Penguins and polar bears have bodies that easily accumulate and store fat under the skin. Today, many people diet to get rid of extra body fat. But long ago, body fat was useful in keeping people alive during cold weather and when food was scarce.

The Spice of Life?

Question: What effect does salt have on houseplant growth?
Hypothesis: High concentrations of salt harm houseplant growth.

Most land plants get the water they need from rain. Rain is fresh water and contains few salts. How would plants react to water that contains increasing amounts of salt?

Materials

- 3 small houseplants (such as a begonia or coleus) of similar size, in identical pots with same type of soil
- table salt
- 2 large containers with covers

Procedure

1. Place the three plants side by side on a sunny or partly sunny windowsill.

2. Prepare two salt solutions. Pour 2 cups (500 mL) tap water into one large container. Add ¼ cup (62.5 mL) salt. Stir until the salt is dissolved. Label the container "12% salt solution." Repeat with the second large container, this time adding 1 cup (250 mL) salt. Label this container "50% salt solution."

3. Label one plant pot "12% salt," the second "50% salt," and the third "Control." The control plant will be watered with plain tap water.

4. Water each plant from its corresponding container of water (12% plant watered from 12% salt solution, etc.). Each plant should get about the same amount of water, about ¼ (62.5 mL) to ½ (125 mL) cup, depending on the size of the pot.

5. Check the three pots once every 2–3 days. Record your observations. If the surface of the soil is dry, give each plant the same amount of water at the same time. Continue to monitor and water your plants for about 1 month, or until you clearly see the effects of salt water on the plants.

Analysis

Most plants cannot use salt water, because salt draws water out of cells. Salt water has the same effect on animals and people. Drinking salt water eventually would kill you because it causes your body cells to lose water and die. Yet some plants live in saltwater environments, such as coastal wetlands or the sea. The cells of these plants are able to get rid of the salt in the water they take in, and use only the fresh water that is left.

Bloom or Bust?

Question: What effect does fertilizer concentration in water have on the growth of freshwater algae?

Hypothesis: Higher concentrations of fertilizer increase algae growth.

Fertilizer is plant food that improves the yield of crops. *Algae* (AL-jee) are tiny, usually one-celled plants. Some algae live in the ocean, some live in fresh water, such as lakes and ponds. When algae grow wildly, they form a *mat,* or bloom, on water. You will determine the effects of different concentrations of fertilizer on freshwater algae.

Materials

- 3 clean, empty quart-size milk cartons
- 2 large containers with lids
- freshwater algae, skimmed from the surface of a pond or lake
- 3 quarts ($\cong$ 3 L) pond or lake water

- 3 plastic shoe storage boxes of the same size, with lids
- synthetic plant fertilizer that can be dissolved in water (available at garden-supply stores)
- toothpick

Procedure

1. Bring the milk cartons and the two lidded containers to a pond or lake. Collect algae in one container. Collect 3 quarts ($\cong$ 3 L) pond or lake water using the milk carton and pour it into the other container. Cover both containers to bring them home.

2. Pour 1 quart ($\cong$ 1 L) pond water into each plastic shoe box.

3. Prepare the fertilizer solution according to the directions on the package. Mix the specified amount of fertilizer (for 1 quart/1 L) into the water in one shoe box. Stir until dissolved. Label this shoe box "1x fertilizer."

4. Mix twice the recommended amount of fertilizer into the second shoe box, and stir until dissolved. Label this shoe box "2x fertilizer." Put no fertilizer in the third shoe box. Label this "Control."

5. Distribute the algae as equally as possible among the three shoe boxes. After 15 minutes, use the toothpick to gently nudge the algae together on the surface of the water (A). Use a ruler to measure the length and width of the algae. Record the measurement. Repeat for the algae in each shoe box.

6. Cover the shoe boxes and set them in a warm place, in indirect sunlight, where they will not be disturbed.

7. Check the shoe boxes every 2 days. Measure the length and width of the algae bloom covering the water's surface. Continue to observe, measure, and monitor the algae bloom in the shoe boxes for at least 2 weeks.

Analysis

Because algae are one-celled plants, fertilizer does not make them grow bigger, but rather speeds up their reproduction. When rain washes fertilizer off farmland and into rivers, most of the fertilizer ends up in coastal and freshwater environments, where it causes algae to reproduce wildly. The result is often huge, harmful algae blooms. The algae use up the oxygen in the water that fish need to breathe. Fertilizer runoff also may cause the rapid reproduction of poisonous algae, leading to toxic algae blooms, sometimes called red tides.

Blow Up

TIME

1–2 hours

Question: How can you show that gases take up space?
Hypothesis: Gases take up space.

When you mix bicarbonate of soda with vinegar, a chemical reaction causes a gas to form. This gas is *carbon dioxide,* which is used to make soda pop. You will show that carbon dioxide takes up so much space, it can blow up a balloon!

Materials

- small glass bottle with a narrow neck
- white vinegar
- funnel
- balloon that fits snugly over mouth of bottle
- bicarbonate of soda (baking soda)

Procedure

1. Make sure the bottle is clean and dry. Carefully fill the bottle ¼ full with white vinegar.

2. Using the funnel, carefully pour the bicarbonate of soda into the balloon. Tap the funnel to get all the bicarbonate into the balloon. Put enough bicarbonate into the balloon to fill it, but not so much that it expands.

3. With the bulb of the balloon hanging down, gently stretch the balloon over the mouth and neck of the bottle (A). When the balloon is secure, quickly lift the bulb directly over the bottle so that the bicarbonate falls into the vinegar. Shake the bottle a bit to mix the bicarbonate and vinegar. A fizzy gas will be produced (B). You will know that the carbon dioxide is expanding and taking up space because it will blow up the balloon.

Analysis

Vinegar is an acid. Bicarbonate of soda is a base. When a base and an acid mix, a chemical reaction occurs, and carbon dioxide is produced. There was not enough room in the bottle for all the gas, so it inflated the balloon.

Bubble, Bubble

TIME

1–2 months

Question: Does acid rain wear away rocks (or building materials) in your area?

Hypothesis: Acid rain does/does not wear away rocks in my area.

Some rocks, such as limestone, contain a base, which reacts when it comes into contact with acid. As a result, the acid wears away the rock. Other kinds of rocks do not contain a base, so they don't react with acid. In this project, you will use the acid in vinegar to determine if the rocks in your area could be affected by acid rain.

Materials

- digging tool
- paper bag
- several medium-size jars with lids, one for each rock
- accurate, sensitive scale
- white vinegar

Procedure

1. Take the digging tool and the paper bag to a nearby park. Dig up as many different kinds of small rocks as you can and put them in the paper bag. Each rock should be small enough to fit in a medium-size jar.

2. At home, wash each rock under running water and a little liquid soap. Rinse the rocks well and let them dry.

3. Wash the jars thoroughly with soap and hot water. Let them dry.

4. Weigh each rock on the scale. Record the exact weight. (You will keep a record of each rock's weight throughout the project.)

5. Place a rock in each jar. Pour enough white vinegar into each jar to cover the rock. Then cover the jars. Note and record if you see any bubbles rising from any of the rocks. If the rock is fizzing, that means it contains limestone (a base).

6. Once a week, weigh each rock on the scale and record the weight. Continue the experiment for 1–2 months for best results.

Analysis

Vinegar is a mild acid. The base in limestone is calcium carbonate. When vinegar comes into contact with limestone, the acid and the base react to produce a gas, and the gas forms bubbles.

Acid rain occurs when factory smokestacks release chemicals. These chemicals react with the water vapor in clouds. If one of these chemicals is sulfur, it will form sulfuric (suhl-FYOOR-ik) acid. The acid falls from the clouds as rain. Acid rain often falls far from its source, because it is carried by winds high above the earth.

Variation

Design a project that tests acid rain's effect on certain building materials. These materials may include rocks, brick, and wood. What is your hypothesis about which building material is best in an area that gets acid rain?

Colorful Carnations

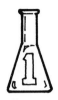

Question: How can capillary action be shown to occur in plants? Do the inner vessels of plants channel liquid to different plant parts?

Hypothesis: The inner vessels of plants use capillary action to move liquid to different parts of a plant.

Plants take in water through their roots. But how does the water get to the plants' leaves? How does it get to the leaves of a tall tree? You will find out how *capillary* (KAP-ih-layr-ee) *action* works. You also will show that vessels inside a plant's stem channel water to different parts of a flower.

Materials

- 2 clear glasses
- 2 different colors of food coloring
- long-stemmed white carnation
- scissors or knife

Procedure

1. Fill the glasses about ¾ full with tap water. Add one food coloring to one glass. Add the other food coloring to the other glass. Use enough food coloring to get a good, strong color in the water. Place the glasses next to each other. Let them sit until the water reaches room temperature.

2. Remove any leaves from the stem of the carnation. Ask an adult to trim the stem to about 13 inches (32.5 cm) long. Have him or her use the scissors to split the stem in half lengthwise to within about 8 inches (20 cm) of the flower (A). Be careful not to crush the stem.

3. Carefully place one half of the stem in one glass, and the other half in the other glass (B). Adjust the glasses so that the stems stay in the water and the flower stands upright between them.

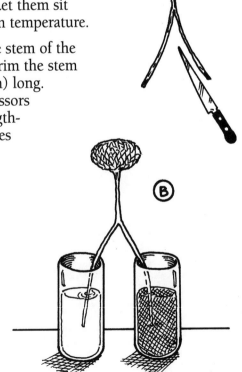

4. Record the time when you put the split stems in the glasses. Check the flower every hour. Does its color change? Record the time when you see the petals begin to take on the color of the water in each glass. Count the number of petals that turn a different color.

Analysis

The colored water traveled all the way up to the flower petals through capillary action. Inside a plant's stem are long, thin tubes, or vessels, made up of cells. Water molecules climb up these cells. As they do, more molecules follow, because water molecules tend to stick to each other (that's why water forms drops). The molecules get so tightly packed in the stem cells that they become strong enough to pull up even more water molecules. The water moves up and up until the whole plant has had enough to drink.

Variation

Do this project using different kinds of flowers or plants. Do different plants move water at different rates? Try this experiment with water at different temperatures. Does temperature affect the rate of capillary action?

For the Birds

Question: Do all birds prefer the same kind of birdseed?
Hypothesis: Different birds prefer different kinds of birdseed.

Perhaps you have seen different kinds of birds at a bird feeder. Do all the birds eat the same seeds? If you put out different kinds of seeds, would you attract different kinds of birds? Do birds, like people and other animals, prefer one kind of food over another?

Materials

- 5 flat plastic plates
- stones, clay, nails, or tacks to anchor the plates; or, large piece of cardboard
- 5 varieties of birdseed (sun-flower seeds; shelled, unsalted peanuts; millet; cracked corn; thistle seeds; or any other)

- field guide to local birds (available at a library or bookstore)

Procedure

1. Place the plates on an outside deck or on a windowsill, about 5 inches (12.5 cm) apart. Anchor the plates using the stones, clay, nails, or tacks. If you are using a large piece of cardboard, glue the plates to one end. Stick this end out a window that opens and closes up and down, not side to side. Close the window on the cardboard and make sure it is held securely in place.

2. Measure 1 cup (250 mL) of each kind of birdseed and place it on a plate. Each plate gets one kind of seed.

3. Over the next 2–3 weeks, record the number of each species of bird that comes to feed at each plate. Note feather color, body size, beak shape, distinct markings, and so on.

Analysis

4. Use the field guide to identify each kind of bird. If necessary, have an adult help you. In your notebook, write the name of each bird species you see. Under each name, keep a daily record of how many birds of each species you see and which type of seed they like to eat.

Different birds eat different seeds. A bird's size and the size and shape of its beak sometimes are clues to the kind of seed it prefers. For example, large birds, such as blue jays, have large, strong beaks. They often prefer to eat large seeds, such as peanuts. Smaller birds, like sparrows, have smaller beaks. They may prefer to eat smaller seeds like sunflower seeds or thistle seeds.

High and Dry

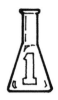

Question: What foods contain the most water?
Hypothesis: Fruits contain more water than other foods.

All fresh foods contain water. That's because all living things must have water to survive. In this project, you will show how the process of *evaporation* (evap-oh-RAY-shun) helps determine which foods contain the most water.

Materials

- test fruits (such as pear, peach, grapes, apple) and vegetables (such as spinach, brussel sprouts, broccoli, potato)
- several empty onion bags (one for each food) or other netting
- twist ties
- knife (optional)
- food scale
- string
- rubber gloves

Procedure

1. If you are using netting, you should have enough to make pouches that can hold each test food. Put one type of food in each bag. Close securely with a twist tie. (**Note:** You can have an adult slice the food to reduce drying time.)

2. Weigh each bag on the food scale and record the weight.

3. With an adult's help, use the string to tie each bag outdoors in a sunny place, such as on a tree limb or clothesline. Hang them high enough so that animals cannot get to them. (**Note:** Do not leave the bags out overnight. Bring them indoors and rehang them the next morning. If it rains, bring the bags in and rehang after the rain has stopped.)

4. Check the bags once a week. Note which foods appear to be drying more quickly. At the end of 2 weeks, the foods should be dry. (Drying time depends on the weather in your area: rainfall, temperature, amount of sunlight, and other factors will affect drying time.)

5. When all the foods appear to be dry, take down the bags. Put on the rubber gloves and weigh each bag again. Record the weight. Compare each food's weight before they were hung and after they dried out. The food that lost the most weight contained the most water.

Analysis

Foods "lose weight" when the water they contain is lost through *evaporation,* a process in which water changes from a liquid to a gas. The heat of the sun caused the water in the food to turn into water vapor. The water vapor escaped through pores in the foods' skin. The plump and juicy foods became dry and shriveled.

Looking for Light

Question: Can plant stems move around obstacles toward a light source?
Hypothesis: Plant stems can move around obstacles toward light.

All plants need light to live. Plants are "programmed" to turn toward a source of light, which in most cases is the sun. In this project, you will find out if plants will react to a light source even if obstacles are placed in their way.

Materials

- vine-type (not bush-type) bean seed
- small bowl
- small flower pot
- potting soil
- scissors
- 2 pieces cardboard
- shoe box with lid
- tape
- plant grow-light or full-spectrum light (optional)

Procedure

1. Soak the bean seed in the small bowl in room-temperature water for 24 hours.

2. Fill the flower pot with potting soil. Plant the bean seed just under the surface. Water the soil thoroughly, but don't soak it. Check the soil every day and keep it moist until the seed sprouts and the seedling grows to about 2 inches (5 cm) tall (A).

3. Cut the two pieces of cardboard to fit inside the shoe box. Cut a window out of the left half of each piece (B).

4. Stand the shoe box on one end. Cut a large window in the center of the top end. Place the pot with the seedling at the bottom of the box. Tape one piece of cardboard 2 inches (5 cm) above the seedling (C).

5. Put the lid on the shoe box and place it in a sunny window or directly under a grow-lamp. Every day, check the plant for water and watch how it is growing.

6. When the plant has grown several inches more, tape the second piece of cardboard a few inches above the first. Make sure its window is opposite the window of the lower piece (D). Put the lid back on and keep the box in the light. Check the plant daily and watch how it grows.

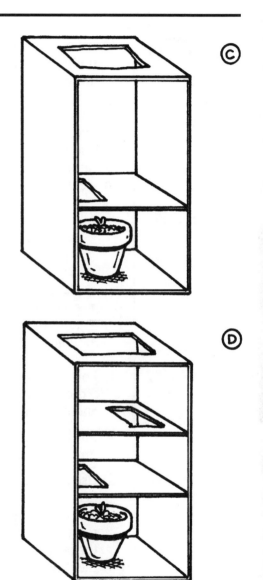

Analysis

The plant should have curved and wound its way through the cardboard windows as it moved toward the light source at the top of the shoe box. This reaction is called *phototropism* (foh-TUH-troh-pizm). A plant will move through almost any obstacle in search of light. Phototropism is essential for plants, because plants use the energy in sunlight to make their own food.

Fat Chance

Question: How can we tell if a food contains saturated or unsaturated fat?
Hypothesis: A chemical reaction will show which foods contain saturated or unsaturated fat.

Saturated fats usually are solid at room temperature. Unsaturated fats, like vegetable oil, are liquid at room temperature. Saturated fats are unhealthful, causing heart disease and other medical problems. Unsaturated fats are not as harmful. You will test different substances to see if they contain saturated or unsaturated fats.

Materials

- test oils or fats (safflower, canola, corn, or other vegetable oil; stick of butter; lard or other animal fat)
- glass jar
- eyedropper
- tincture of iodine
- large pot

- pot holder
- timer, clock, or watch
- test foods (optional): ground beef, banana, milk, ice cream
Note: Do not test starchy foods, such as bread, baked goods, or potatoes.

Procedure

1. Pour 1 ounce (31.25 mL) of a test oil or fat into the glass jar. Add 5 drops iodine. Stir well. Record the time you made the mixture and its appearance.

2. Put 2 inches (5 cm) water into the pot. Have an adult heat the water until it boils. Remove the pot from the heat.

3. Use the pot holder to carefully place the jar inside the pot (A). Leave the jar for 10 minutes, checking the contents every 2 minutes and recording your observations each time. When the water is at room temperature, take out the jar. Dispose of the oil and wash the jar thoroughly with detergent and water. (Do not pour oil down the drain.)

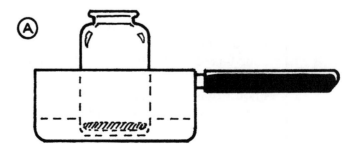

Ⓐ

WARNING

Do not drink iodine. It is a poison.

4. Repeat steps 1 through 3 for each oil or fat you are testing.

5. If you wish, repeat steps 1 through 3 for each test food. Record the amount of each food. Keep the amounts small: 1 teaspoon (5 mL) each.

Analysis

When iodine is heated with a fat, it binds chemically with the fat molecules. The more unsaturated a fat is, the more iodine will bond with it. If some of the fats or oils you tested were unsaturated, the reddish-brown iodine in the jar should have disappeared as the iodine bonded with the fat molecules. The quicker the iodine disappears, the more unsaturated the fat is. If the iodine does not disappear, that substance contains saturated fat.

Dairy Glue

Question: Does glue made from milk work as well as commercial (store-bought) glue?

Hypothesis: Glue made from milk will work as well as commercial glue.

Milk contains many nutrients, such as vitamin D and calcium. It also contains a substance that can be used to make glue. In this project, you will compare milk glue with commercial glue.

Materials

- skim milk
- enamel cooking pot
- white vinegar
- container with lid (for milk glue)
- strainer or colander
- bowl
- bicarbonate of soda (baking soda)

- sheets of paper, pieces of wood, small sheets of metal (aluminum foil, etc.)
- commercial glues for testing (white glue, contact cement, etc.)

Procedure

1. Measure 2 cups (500 mL) skim milk and pour it into the pot. Add 6 tablespoons (90 mL) white vinegar.

2. Have an adult heat the mixture slowly, stirring continuously. When the milk begins to *curdle,* or form small lumps, remove the pot from the heat. Continue to stir until the curdling stops.

3. Pour the mixture into the container and wash out the pot. Let the mixture sit for several hours, or until the curdled part sinks to the bottom.

4. When the curds have sunk, pour off the liquid (whey). (You do not need to keep the liquid.) You have separated the curds and whey. Let the mixture sit again for a few hours.

5. Put the curds in a strainer over a bowl until they drain completely (A).

Ⓐ

6. Place the strained curds back in the pot. Mix in ¼ cup (62.5 mL) water and 1 tablespoon (15 mL) bicarbonate (B). (Note the bubbles that may form.) This is your milk glue. Put the glue back into the container.

7. Use a spoon to smear some milk glue on a sheet of paper. Stick another sheet of paper to it. Try to separate the sheets. Record what happens.

8. Repeat step 7 using a commercial glue. Record what happens with each glue tested.

9. Test your milk glue and commercial glues on other materials. Record your results. Does milk glue work as well or last as long as commercial glue on these materials? At your science fair display, keep different materials and glues handy so that visitors can try the experiment.

Analysis

Milk contains casein, which has gluelike properties when it is removed from the liquid part of milk. (See "Plastic Fantastic!" on page 19.) In liquid form, casein can be used in paint. In solid form, it can be used to make buttons and other objects. Vinegar, an acid, reacts chemically with milk to make it sour and curdle. When you added baking soda—a base—you created another chemical reaction that released gas that formed glue. Your milk glue is similar to commercial white glue, but it is different from cement and other commercial glues that may work better on materials other than paper.

Sound Off!

Question: How does a magnet affect audiotape?
Hypothesis: A magnet will erase sound recorded on an audiotape cassette.

Recording tape—whether it is videotape or audiotape—is made from a magnetized strip of material. You already know that magnets affect each other. How will they affect the sound on a magnetic audiotape?

Materials

- tape recorder
- 30-minute (or less) blank cassette
- strong magnet, large enough to be held easily

Procedure

1. Put the blank cassette in the recorder and record a short message in your own voice. Stop the tape and rewind it to the beginning. Play the recording and make sure it is loud and clear. Stop the tape. Do not rewind it. Take the cassette out of the recorder.

2. Have a helper use a fingernail to turn the tiny "teeth" on the cassette, rewinding it back to the beginning (A). Hold the magnet directly against the tape until the tape is completely rewound.

3. Put down the magnet. Place the tape back into the recorder. Press PLAY. Listen to the sound. How did the magnet affect your recorded voice?

Analysis

The tiny magnetic particles on magnetic tape start out scattered. When you record your voice or any sound, the built-in microphone in the tape recorder changes the sound vibrations in your voice into an electrical current. This current moves magnets inside the recorder. The magnets rearrange the particles on the tape in a way that matches the sound of your voice. When you run a magnet over a recorded tape, the magnet scatters the tape particles again, and the sound on the tape is erased.

Variation

Does the magnet have to touch the recorded tape in order to erase it? Repeat the experiment holding the magnet at different distances from the recorded tape. Can a magnet arrange the particles on a blank tape to make sounds? Try moving the magnet around a blank tape at different distances. Then play the tape.

For your science fair project, have a magnet, a tape recorder, and blank tapes at your display. Allow visitors to record a message, then use the magnet to try to erase it.

Pump Up the Volume

Question: How does sound (noise) affect the ability to concentrate and remember?

Hypothesis: Loud sound will hinder the ability to concentrate and remember.

You may like to listen to rock music on the radio while you are doing your homework. If the music is loud, does it affect your concentration and your ability to remember what you studied?

Materials

- 2 reading passages (see step 1 below)
- paper and pen or pencil
- music tape and tape player
- several volunteers

Procedure

1. Select two reading passages of about 250 words each. They should be at the reading level for your grade and contain specific information (names, places, dates, events).

2. Write out five questions for each passage. The questions should refer to specific information in the passage.

3. Choose a rock music tape you like or one that is popular. Select one track to play. Before you begin, play the tape for yourself at a low volume and mark this spot on the volume dial. This is your low-volume setting. Then play the same track at a high volume and mark the spot on the dial. This is your high-volume setting. Test your volunteers with the volume set only to these two marks.

4. Have a volunteer read the first passage silently while you play the tape at the low volume. Ask him the five questions about this passage and record the number of questions answered correctly.

5. Play the same track at the high volume while the volunteer reads the second passage. Ask the five questions about this passage and record the number of questions answered correctly.

6. Test as many volunteers as you can. Create tables and graphs of your results.

Analysis

It is more difficult for the brain to focus on information gained through one sense (vision) when another sense (hearing) is being overwhelmed. Though your eyes can see the words written on a page, your brain has more trouble retaining the information when it is being bombarded by loud noise.

Blind Spot

Question: Is the blind spot in the human eye the same for all people?
Hypothesis: The blind spot is/is not the same for all people.

You may have heard that cars have a "blind spot," an area that blocks other cars from the driver's vision. The human eye has a blind spot, too. You will find the approximate size of this blind spot.

Materials

- blank white index card, 3 x 5 inches (7.5 x 12.5 cm)
- black felt-tip marker
- yardstick or meter stick

Procedure

1. Use the marker to make a solid dot on the left side of the index card and an X on the right side of the card. The dot and the X should be no more than ½ inch (1.25 cm) high. They should be about ½ inch (1.25 cm) from each edge and centered vertically.

2. Hold the yardstick straight out in front of your nose with one hand. Hold the card in the other hand with the X on the right. Center the card on the yardstick at arm's length.

3. Close your right eye. Look directly at the X with your left eye. You should be able to see both the X and the dot.

4. Slowly slide the card along the yardstick toward your nose (A). Keep your right eye closed and your left eye on the X. The dot should still be in your field of vision.

5. When the dot disappears from your field of vision, or almost disappears, stop moving the card. Record the spot on the yardstick (round it up to the nearest ⅛ inch or centimeter).

6. From this spot, continue moving the card, keeping your right eye closed. When the dot reappears, stop moving the card again. Record this spot. The area between the two spots is the size of your left eye's blind spot.

7. Now, test your right eye's blind spot. Repeat the steps above, but close your left eye and focus on the dot—not the X—with your right eye.

Analysis

8. Try this experiment with different volunteers: girls, boys, parents, grandparents. Is the size of the blind spot the same for all people?

The optic nerve in your eye carries light signals from your eye to the brain, where they are interpreted as images. The optic nerve passes through one spot where your eye is not sensitive to light. This is the blind spot. The number of inches (centimeters) you measured between the two spots is the size of the blind spot. Did you find that different people have different-size blind spots? Graph your results and draw conclusions.

Let's Stick Together

Question: What materials are best at moving water through capillary action?

Hypothesis: Natural, fuzzy fibers are best at moving water using capillary action.

The molecules that make up water tend to stick to each other. (See "Colorful Carnations," page 74.) If water is absorbed by a fabric, the molecules in front pull up those behind. This is how the water "soaks into" a fabric. You will find out which fabrics absorb water the best.

Materials

- small bowls, one for each fabric
- various colors of food coloring
- different kinds of WHITE fabric (cotton, wool, polyester, nylon, etc.)
- scissors

Procedure

1. Put ½ cup (125 mL) water into each bowl. Stir in a different food coloring to each bowl, enough to make a strong color.

2. Have an adult cut a narrow strip from each fabric, ½ inch (1.25 cm) wide and 12 inches (30 cm) long. Wet each strip with water. Place one end into each bowl. At least 2 inches (5 cm) should be in the liquid, or enough so that the end does not come out of the bowl. Let the other end hang out onto the tabletop (A).

3. Record each kind of fabric you are testing. Under each fabric, note the time you placed the strip in the bowl of colored water.

4. Check the strips every half hour for 3 hours. Note which have color moving through them.

5. At the end of 3 hours, remove each strip and set it flat on the table. Measure how much of the strip absorbed the colored water. Record your data. Which fabric strip had the longest streak of color?

Analysis

Fabric is made of fibers, which contain threads with tiny, tubelike spaces in between. When water molecules move through these spaces, they are absorbed by the fabric. Capillary action causes the molecules to pull other molecules through the fabric until all the spaces are filled with water.

Variation

Does temperature affect capillary action? Mix the food coloring with hot water. (Keep the water in each bowl hot by adding hot water as needed.) Record the temperature of the water you are using. Also, record the rate at which different fabrics absorb hot water.

Heavy Metal

Question: What common substance has the greatest density?
Hypothesis: Metals are denser than nonmetal substances.

You know that a bucket of water weighs more than a bucket of feathers. That's because water is *denser,* or weighs more, because it is more compact than feathers. What substances are the most dense?

Materials

- clean, 1-liter plastic soda bottle
- sharp knife
- plastic tube, about 6 inches (15 cm) long (available at hardware stores)
- modeling clay
- test objects (iron nail, key, wooden, ceramic, plastic objects)
- food scale
- calculator (optional)

Procedure

1. Ask an adult to cut off the top of the soda bottle. Use the knife to make a hole 3 inches (7.5 cm) below the rim. The hole should be just big enough to fit the plastic tube.

2. Insert the plastic tube into the hole so that only the tip is inside the bottle. Seal the hole around the tube with clay to make it watertight (A).

3. Put a measuring cup under the other end of the tube. Fill the bottle with water just until it pours out of the tube and into the cup (B). Discard the water in the cup, and put the cup back under the tube.

4. To measure the density of an object, immerse it in the water in the bottle. As the water level rises, some of it will drain out of the tube and into the cup. Record how much water is in the cup. Remove the object from the bottle and weigh it on the food scale.

5. Now, divide the object's weight by the amount of water in the measuring cup. This number is the object's density. Record it in your notebook.

6. Repeat steps 4 and 5 for each object. Add water to the bottle before each test by repeating step 3. Use the same unit of measure for all objects (ounces or milliliters of water displaced, ounces or grams of weight).

Analysis

Density is the number of atoms that are packed into a given space in a substance. The closer together the atoms are, the denser the substance is. Water has 1,000 more atoms in a given space than air does. Gold is about 20 times denser than water. Gases are less dense than liquids, which are less dense than solids.

Index